DEALING WITH STRONGHOLDS

PART FOUR OF THE DEVELOPING GIFTS AND
SKILLS SERIES

DR. HENDRIK J VORSTER

CONTENTS

DEALING WITH STRONGHOLDS
PART FOUR OF THE DEVELOPING GIFTS AND SKILLS SERIES

-- Disciple Manual --

Dealing with Strongholds
Part Four of the Developing Gifts and Skills Series
(Disciple Manual)
By Dr. Hendrik J. Vorster

For more copies and information please visit and write to us at: www. churchplantinginstitute.com
resources@churchplantinginstitute.com

ISBN 978-1-955923-16-3

PART I

DEALING WITH STRONGHOLDS

Part Four of the Developing Gifts and Skills Series

1

INTRODUCTION
SESSION ONE

C hrist paid a deer price that we could be free from slavery to sin. To ensure that we grow, develop and bring into fruit the gracious work of the Holy Spirit in us, we need to weed out those encumbrances that will keep us from seeing our full harvest. Christ set us free from sin and slavery. He broke the yoke of slavery to sin; however, we learn from John that young believers overcome the evil one by applying the Blood of the Lamb and standing on the Truth of God's Word.

This weekend is about overcoming the evil one. This weekend is about taking the yoke off and walking away with the Freedom Christ brought to us.

> *Galatians 5:1 (NIV) Freedom in Christ "1 It is for freedom that Christ has set us free. Stand firm, then, and do not let yourselves be burdened again by a yoke of slavery."*

> *1 John 2:13-14 (NIV) "13 I am writing to you, fathers, because you know him who is from the beginning. I am writing to you, young men, **because you have overcome the evil one.** 14 I write to you, dear children, because you know the Father. I write to*

> *you, fathers, because you know him who is from the beginning.*
> *I write to you, **young men, because you are strong, and the***
> ***word of God lives in you, and you have overcome the evil one.***"

> *Revelation 12:11 "**11 They triumphed over him by the blood of the***
> ***Lamb and by the word of their testimony;** they did not love*
> *their lives so much as to shrink from death.*"

Every time we read the Word, every time we pray, every time we sow seeds of the Gospel by sharing our testimony, every time we sow financial seed, we plant towards a spiritual harvest. Jesus promised that we could expect a 30, 60 or 100-fold harvest if we have been planted in the right soil, grown roots and weeded out of our lives those things that might choke the fruit from coming into harvest.

> ***Matthew 13:22 (NKJV),*** "*Now he who received seed among the*
> *thorns is he who hears the word, and the cares of this world and*
> *the deceitfulness of riches choke the word, and he becomes*
> *unfruitful.*"

This course is designed to remove those obvious, and sometimes not so obvious, encroaching and encumbering habits, aptitudes, pursuits, and practices that will inhibit our growth and enjoyment of the harvest, of our service unto the Lord.

The "_____ *of the world, deceitfulness of* _____, *and* _____" often consume much needed nourishment away that would have seen our harvest and expected outcome realised. Lingering aptitudes, such as undealt hurt, fear, unforgiveness, rejection, and resentment, often keep us from reaching our Promised Land.

Where we observe these things remaining in our disciples' lives, we take time during this weekend encounter to deal with those decisively. This course is also designed to set our affections on the right things. Setting your affections on the wrong things will most certainly distract you from the purposes of God.

The Bible outlines how these things affect us in the Parable of the Sower, in Matthew 13. Interestingly, thorns only required removal at this stage of the seed's growth, as it posed a threat when it is about to reproduce. Therefore, it makes sense that once you've developed spiritual values and disciplines, you must get rid of these "thorns" that might keep you from being fruitful.

The Bible also outlines those things that kept Israel from reaching their Promised land; they were **unbelief and disobedience**. These two thorns still keep good people out of their promised land today. Through the years we have seen the terrible impact *fear, doubt and unbelief* has on people, but also the devastation for those who continued with **unforgiveness and bitterness**.

Finally, we will look at **faith and obedience** as sure tenets to ensure our successful possession of the Full Harvest and Good Land God promised us.

2

CARES OF THE WORLD, DECEITFULNESS OF RICHES, AND PRIDE

SESSION TWO

L et us look at each of these areas individually during this session.

CARES OF THE WORLD

Right from the outset of Jesus' teachings he addressed the *"cares of the world"* as a weed which we need to guard ourselves against, and which we should root out by placing our complete trust and faith in God. At its core the *"cares of the world"* challenges the Source of our _____, and His ability to _____ us.

> *Matthew 13:22 (NKJV), "Now he who received seed among the thorns is he who hears the word, and **the cares of this world** and the deceitfulness of riches choke the word, and he becomes unfruitful."*

Cares are concerns that we worry about. Some people are even known are **"worry-ers."** They worry about everything. What Jesus was saying in this Parable was that the "cares of the world" robs us from seeing our expected _____, and even can cause us to become _____. It challenges us greatly when we worked for something and then don't get to see the end result of it, or see the project through to completion, or enjoy the fruit of our hard labour or investment.

What do the world care about? They care about what we eat, drink and wear. They care about position, possessions, and their pride drives them to have more, keep more, and self-sustain more.

> *Matthew 6:25-34 Do Not Worry "Therefore, I tell you, do not worry about your life, what you will eat or drink; or about your body, what you will wear. Is not life more important than food, and the body more important than clothes? Look at the birds of the air; they do not sow or reap or store away in barns, and yet your heavenly Father feeds them. Are you not much more valuable than they? Who of you by worrying can add a single hour to his life? And why do you worry about clothes? See how the lilies of the field grow. They do not labor or spin. Yet I tell you that not even Solomon in all his splendor was dressed like one of these. If that is how God clothes the grass of the field, which is here today and tomorrow is thrown into the fire, will he not much more clothe you, O you of little faith? So do not worry, saying, 'What shall we eat?' or 'What shall we drink?' or 'What shall we wear?' For the pagans run after all these things, and your heavenly Father knows that you need them. But seek first his kingdom and his righteousness, and all these things will be given to you as well. Therefore, do not worry about tomorrow, for tomorrow will worry about itself. Each day has enough trouble of its own."*

More often, than not, the things people worry about are shared in this message of Jesus. God is our source. He is the One who feeds us, clothes us and protects us.

Israel, at one point, thought that it was their strength that brought them the victories, the provisions and the security they treasured, but the Lord sternly reminded them that it was His Power that accomplished all that for them. These encapsulate the essentials of the cares and concerns people carry with them on a daily basis, the very thing the Lord teaches us not to do.

> Deuteronomy 8:10-18 *"When you have eaten and are satisfied, praise the Lord your God for the good land he has given you. 11* **Be careful that you do not forget the Lord your God, failing to observe his commands, his laws and his decrees that I am giving you this day. 12 Otherwise, when you eat and are satisfied, when you build fine houses and settle down, 13 and when your herds and flocks grow large and your silver and gold increase and all you have is multiplied, 14 then your heart will become proud and you will forget the Lord your God,** *who brought you out of Egypt, out of the land of slavery. 15 He led you through the vast and dreadful desert, that thirsty and waterless land, with its venomous snakes and scorpions. He brought you water out of hard rock. 16 He gave you manna to eat in the desert, something your fathers had never known, to humble and to test you so that in the end it might go well with you. 17 You may say to yourself,* **"My power and the strength of my hands have produced this wealth for me."** *18* **But remember the Lord your God, for it is he who gives you the ability to produce wealth, and so confirms his covenant,** *which he swore to your forefathers, as it is today."*

We are encouraged to not be anxious about anything since God is our Provider, Protector and the One who blesses us.

> *1 Peter 5:7 Cast all your anxiety on him because he cares for you.*

> *Psalms 55:22 Cast your cares on the Lord and he will sustain you; he will never let the righteous fall.*

Today we declare that God is our strength, it is He who gives us the ability to produce wealth! We also declare that it is He who saved us and brought us into a good land, flowing with Milk and Honey. It is He who gives us victories. It is He who enables us to build houses and to study and to succeed in business. It is He who enables us to have the privileges we currently enjoy. We declare our gratitude to Him for the clothes we are able to wear, the food we are able to eat, and the drinks we are able to drink.

Take a moment and declare your complete gratitude and trust in Him as the source of your life!

Deceitfulness of riches

Now, this portion also addresses the second part of the weeds that robs us from our intended and expected harvest, and that is the *"deceitfulness of _____."* The Israelites was forewarned that when their gold and silver increases, that they needed to remind themselves that it was indeed the Lord who gave them these riches and that it was not their own goodness or ability that gave it to them.

People often have a false sense of security built around their wealth and _____.

People think that their _____ secures them from pandemics, misfortune or even poverty, however, we are warned against such false thinking.

> *Deuteronomy 8:17 You may say to yourself, "My power and the strength of my hands have produced this wealth for me." 18 But remember the Lord your God, for it is he who gives you the ability to produce wealth, and so confirms his covenant, which he swore to your forefathers, as it is today.*

These words stand as an eternal warning and guidance for all those who will place their trust in their wealth.

The Lord is the One who gives us _____ and He is the One who allows us to _____.

We should eternally be grateful when He grants us such blessings to be enjoyed.

> *1 Samuel 2:7 The Lord sends poverty and wealth; he humbles, and he exalts.*

> *Proverbs 8:18 With me are riches and honor, enduring wealth and prosperity.*

God is the source of all riches, wealth and prosperity. We will be wise to always remember from whom we have received such blessings. The defining principle is to remain grateful and not to become proud and arrogant, and to forget the Lord. We have what we have because of His great Grace. The Bible teaches us that it is through His blessing that we increase our wealth.

> *Proverbs 10:22 (NIV) The blessing of the Lord brings wealth, and he adds no trouble to it.*

The Apostle Paul taught Timothy to **"teach those who are rich"** to not put their hope in their wealth, but to put their hope in God. If we remain dependent on God, even though He has given us great wealth, then we will most certainly see the Good seed sown into our lives come into producing a multiplied harvest. It is this self-reliance, self-sufficiency and independence that deceives us, and eventually chokes the fruit from producing and multiplying.

> *1 Timothy 6:17-19 (NIV) Command those who are rich in this present world not to be arrogant nor to put their hope in wealth, which is so uncertain, but to put their hope in God, who richly provides us with everything for our enjoyment. 18 Command them to do good, to be rich in good deeds, and to be generous and willing to share. 19 In this way they will lay up treasure for themselves as a firm foundation for the coming age, so that they may take hold of the life that is truly life.*

The Apostle Paul also taught that people who become rich often find themselves enticed by foolish and harmful desires which plunge them into ruin and destruction. Many people wander away from their faith and pierce themselves with many griefs, as a result of pursuing these evil desires and pleasures. Our attention is drawn to the *"deceitfulness of riches,"* in as far as it can make us forget who granted us the blessings, and lead us to a false sense of security.

> *1 Timothy 6:9-10 (NIV) People who want to get rich fall into temptation and a trap and into many foolish and harmful desires that plunge men into ruin and destruction. For the love of money is a root of all kinds of evil. Some people, eager for money, have wandered from the faith and pierced themselves with many griefs.*

The desire and dream God have for us is known: He desires to give us an expected end. The very things we work towards in our faith, that's the fruit God desires for us to bear. The Lord desires for us to be fruitful and to multiply greatly and to see the expected end of our faith pursuits.

> **Riches bring with it a sense of false security that we will be _____ even if bad things happen to us.**

This false security chokes us from fruitfulness, whereas gratefulness, reliance and dependency on God keeps the expectations alive, to see fruit on our labour. This is the very thing God constantly exhorts and encourages us towards.

> *Jeremiah 29:11 (KJV) For I know the thoughts that I think toward you, saith the Lord, thoughts of peace, and not of evil, **to give you an expected end.***

> *Galatians 6:9 (NIV) 9 Let us not become weary in doing good, for at the proper time we will reap a harvest if we do not give up.*

Pride

Another area which often chokes our fruitfulness is pride.

- *Pride is that self-esteemed attitude of vein* _____.
- Pride can be described as that conceited and over-perceived value of one's importance or stature.
- Pride is that pre-occupation with self-care, caring only about yourself and your own interest.

Since the time Satan was cast out of the presence of God because of his pride, people have fallen prey to pride, and it too kept them from seeing their fruitful multiplication.

Ezekiel 28:2 (NIV) *"Son of man, say to the ruler of Tyre, This is what the Sovereign Lord says: 'In **the pride of your heart you say**, I am a god; I sit on the throne of a god in the heart of the seas. But you are a man and not a god, though you think you are as wise as a god.'"*

Ezekiel 28:4 (NIV) *By your wisdom and understanding you have gained wealth for yourself and amassed gold and silver in your treasuries. 5 By your great skill in trading you have increased your wealth, and **because of your wealth your heart has grown proud.***

Ezekiel 28:17
Your heart became proud *on account of your beauty, and you corrupted your wisdom because of your splendor. **So, I threw you to the earth;** I made a spectacle of you before kings.*

Satan's pride cost him his privileged position in Heaven. The Bible teaches us to guard against pride.

*Proverbs 16:18 (NIV) **Pride goes before destruction**, And a haughty
  spirit before a fall.*

Pride will most certainly keep us away from fruitfulness. If pride is
not of the Father, then pride should not live in us if we desire fruitfulness. The Apostle John, in his first pastoral letter, outline the very
things that is of the world, but more importantly, those things that are
not of the Father. As people who are grafted in the "**Vine**," we draw
our sap from the Nature of our Heavenly Father.

*1 John 2:16 (KJV) For all that is in the world—the lust of the flesh,
  the lust of the eyes, **and the pride of life**—is not of the Father
  but is of the world.*

The New International Version defines this *"pride"* as *"**the boasting
of what he has and does**."* You can spend a few minutes with someone
and quickly know how much pride exist.

*1 John 2:16-17 (NIV) For everything in the world—the cravings of
  sinful man, the lust of his eyes and **the boasting of what he has
  and does**—comes not from the Father but from the world. 17 The
  world and its desires pass away, but the man who does the will
  of God lives forever.*

In Jesus' message in John 15 on the Vine, the branches and the
fruit, we learn that there is a direct correlation between our connect-
edness to Christ, as the Vine, and the fruit we bear. If pride does not
come from the Father, then drawing our sap from pride will not
produce the fruit we desire to bear in our lives.

If pride got Satan kicked out of Heaven, how much more will it
keep us from God's Presence?

In Conclusion

Search your heart and dispose of any and all pride in your life. Our pursuit through this course is to help you to bring the good seed of the Word, sown into your life, come into a fruitful harvest. What we learnt in this session is how that the cares of this world, the deceitfulness of riches, and pride are those aptitudes that choke the seed from becoming and producing a multiplied harvest.

Assimilation Sheet for
Cares of the World, deceitfulness of riches, and pride.

1. Complete the sentence. *At its core the "cares of the world" challenges the Source of our _____, and His ability to _____ us.*

2. How will the cares of the world leave us with our expectations?
_____

3. What are the cares of the world? _____
_____
_____

4. Which Scriptures best defines, and addresses the Cares of the world to you? _____
_____
_____

5. Complete this sentence. *People think that their _____ secures them from pandemics, misfortune or even poverty, however, we are warned against such false thinking.*

6. Complete the sentence. *People often have a false sense of security built around their wealth and _____.*

7. Complete this sentence. *The Lord is the One who gives us _____ and He is the One who allows us to _____.*

8. Which Scriptures best guides us to think soundly about treasures, riches and wealth? _____
_____
_____

9. Complete the sentence. *Pride is that self-esteemed attitude of vein _____.*

10. What impact did pride have on Satan? _____
_____
_____

11. Which Scriptures warns us against the impact of Pride?
_____

12. Complete the sentence. *Pride will most certainly keep us away from _____.*

3

FEAR AND UNBELIEF

SESSION THREE

Fear and _____ are two enemies that can keep us from seeing the fruit of our labour. These two war against the good seed sown in us. This session is about identifying *fear and unbelief* in our hearts, and to displace them with *faith and obedience* so that we will reap our harvest.

FEAR

Fear is a thistle and thorn that keep many believers from reaping their expected harvest. Fear can keep us out of our Promised land. We are constantly confronted with circumstances which call on us to fear or to face by faith. The New Testament teaches us a powerful principle to remember, and that is that God did not give us a Spirit of fear.

> *2 Timothy 1:7 (KJV) [7] For God hath not given us **the spirit of** _____; but of power, and of love, and of a sound mind.*

The Spirit of the Lord is a Spirit of Love, Power and a Sound mind, yet many, even believers, struggle with a Spirit of fear tormenting them. *Living with Fear is not from God.* I pray that you will know the truth and allow the truth of God's Word to flood your soul today that you can be free from fear and filled with faith and hope.

> *John 8:32* (KJV) "*Then you will know the truth, and the truth will set you free.*"

The King James Bible record **63** instances where the Lord commands His followers to "*fear not.*" The NIV records **107** instances where the Lord says: "***Do not be afraid.***"

The Bible challenges us to not give way to fear, but to live by faith.

Whenever we are faced with a challenge, **we have a choice** to make, either give in to the spirit of fear or face it by faith.

Unbelief

_____ is that act of embracing one's fears and doubt over against the promises of God. Doubt and unbelief kept the Israelites, whom God delivered out of the hands of the mighty Egyptian Rulers' might, out of their Promised land.

> *Hebrews 3:19* (KJV) *So we see that they were not able to enter, because of their unbelief.*

Unbelief is rife in so many people, no wonder that so few people reach their promised land. You can quickly detect unbelief when you listen to people. It is not uncommon to hear people say:"*I don't believe that.*" Though they might be speaking about everyday things, they have become accustomed to constantly stating what they don't believe as apposed to stating what they belief. This become systemic of How they act and respond to life in general. As

Believers we are called to live by faith, in other words, by what we believe.

The Old Testament present to us a number of wonderful examples to which many of us can relate in our present circumstances.

Hagar

The first is that of Hagar, a servant girl, without rights or means for justice in her precarious situation. She had a child with her master, and now the wife of the master threw her out to fend for herself and her son. Even though Sarai was a willing part to this original arrangement with Hagar having a child with Abram, it spiralled out of control and sanity once Ismael was born.

> *Genesis 16:2, 4 (NIV) "so, she said to Abram, 'The Lord has kept me from having children. Go, sleep with my maidservant; perhaps I can build a family through her.' Abram agreed to what Sarai said. 4 He slept with Hagar, and she conceived. When she knew she was pregnant, she began to despise her mistress."*

This pregnancy and despising by Hagar infuriated Sarai that she got rid of her with Abram's consent.

> *Genesis 16:6 (NIV) "Your servant is in your hands," Abram said. "Do with her whatever you think best." Then Sarai mistreated Hagar; so she fled from her.*

After the Angel of the Lord met her, she returned into that hostile situation, but 14 years later when Isaac was born, she was finally ousted from the household.

> *Genesis 21:8 (NIV) The child grew and was weaned, and on the day Isaac was weaned Abraham held a great feast. 9 But Sarah saw that the son whom Hagar the Egyptian had borne to Abraham was mocking, 10 and she said to Abraham, "Get rid of that slave*

woman and her son, for that slave woman's son will never
share in the inheritance with my son Isaac." 11 The matter
distressed Abraham greatly because it concerned his son.

This matter greatly, and rightly, distressed Abraham. He had to send his son, Ismael, and the mother of his son away. I am sure he too was anxious about their welfare. What blessed me from this portion is that God saw his distress and comforted him prior to him sending them off. God has a good plan for each one of us, even though in our distress we might not see it, He has a plan for each of our lives.

> *Genesis 21:12 (NIV) But God said to him, "Do not be so distressed*
> *about the boy and your maidservant. Listen to whatever Sarah*
> *tells you, because it is through Isaac that your offspring will be*
> *reckoned. 13 I will make the son of the maidservant into a*
> *nation also, because he is your offspring."*

Hagar went away with her son and wandered around until their provisions was up. In her desperation she put her son down in a place where she could not hear his cries and sat down and wept out of pure distress and destitution.

> *Genesis 21:17 (NIV) God heard the boy crying, and the angel of God*
> *called to Hagar from heaven and said to her, "What is the*
> *matter, Hagar? Do not be afraid; God has heard the boy crying*
> *as he lies there.*

Every time Hagar found herself in this desperation the Word of God tells us that God saw and heard her.

> **"Fear grips our hearts because we think that God does not _____**
> **or _____ the desperation of our circumstances."**

Before the Lord gave her an outcome to her desperation, He first required of her to take a step in obedience and faith. She had to lift her son up and take him by the hand. Once she did, the Word of God tell us that God opened her eyes and she saw the well of water. God also gave her a wonderful promise of her son's future well-being.

> *Genesis 21:18* (NIV) *"Lift the boy up and take him by the hand, for I will make him into a great nation." 19 Then God opened her eyes and she saw a well of water. So she went and filled the skin with water and gave the boy a drink. 20 God was with the boy as he grew up. He lived in the desert and became an archer.*

This situation plays itself out in modern society daily: girls become pregnant with the children of their employers, bosses, or simply people more powerful and of greater standing than them, and then when their pregnancy becomes known, are thrown out to fend for themselves. Even mentioning it sends up shivers up my spine. Just the thought of the desperation, the injustice, and the cruelty is enough to propel even the kindest into becoming an activist for human rights.

The truth is that those to whom such injustices happen are often filled with fear and anxiety, and rightly so, wouldn't you? I can almost feel their fear and anxiety. The desperation of the predicament you find yourself in. *What is going to happen to me? What is going to happen with my child? How am I going to live? What shall we eat? Where can we go? Where will we live? What will people say?* These are just some of the many questions that I think people in such desperations find themselves asking.

What is important to know from this desperate situation is that; **God hears, God sees, and God will make a way** where there seems to be no way or outcome.

> *Genesis 21:17* (NIV) *God heard the boy crying, and the angel of God called to Hagar from heaven and said to her, "What is the matter, Hagar?* **Do not be afraid***; God has heard the boy crying as he lies there.*

The Lord answered her with those tremendously comforting words: "**Do not be afraid!**" Fear grips even the most toughest of us. May we take courage from how the Lord intervened in the desperation of Hagar.

Isaac

During Isaac's journeys there was a great famine in the land.

> *Genesis 26:1 (NIV) Now there was a famine in the land—besides the earlier famine of Abraham's time—and Isaac went to Abimelech king of the Philistines in Gerar.*

Isaac was a herdsman with lots of livestock, so the onset of a famine would bring within him anxiety and fear for what the future holds for him and his livestock. The amazing thing is that, no sooner was the consideration uttered in Isaac's heart, when God gave him, not just guidance and instruction as to what to do, but also a wonderful confirmation of the Promise He first gave to his Father Abraham. This Promise of God not just secured guidance for the present challenge they faced but also secured hope for the future. The key response of Isaac in his distress is seen in verse 6 when the Word says: "**So Isaac stayed.**" He overcame a terrible fearful situation by obeying the directive of the Lord.

> *Genesis 26:2 (NIV) "The Lord appeared to Isaac and said, 'Do not go down to Egypt; live in the land where I tell you to live. 3 Stay in this land for a while, and I will be with you and will bless you. For to you and your descendants I will give all these lands and will confirm the oath I swore to your father Abraham. 4 I will make your descendants as numerous as the stars in the sky and will give them all these lands, and through your offspring all nations on earth will be blessed, 5 because Abraham obeyed me and kept my requirements, my commands, my decrees and my laws.' 6 So Isaac stayed in Gerar."*

Isaac then faced a challenge with Abimelech, since he feared for his life since he anticipated that the men of the city might kill him for his beautiful wife, Rebekah. In his fear he told everyone that she was his sister, when in fact she was his wife. When he was found out by the king, he even feared more for his life, but in his fear, God came and consoled him again.

> *Genesis 26:9 (NIV) "So Abimelech summoned Isaac and said, 'She is really your wife! Why did you say, 'She is my sister'? Isaac answered him, 'Because I thought I might lose my life on account of her.'"*

Staying in obedience, even though the circumstances seemed to stack up against him, kept Isaac in a position where God could bring great blessings upon him. ***The place where he feared for his life is the very place where God brought great increase upon Isaac.*** Genesis 26 verses 12 and onwards tell us how God prospered him.

> *Genesis 26:12 (NIV) Isaac planted crops in that land and the same year reaped a hundredfold, because the Lord blessed him. 13 The man became rich, and his wealth continued to grow until he became very wealthy.*

His obedience to stay where God wanted him, even though the natural circumstances called him to move and to be confronted with fearing for his life, he stayed, and God rewarded his faith and obedience by prospering him greatly.

He became so prosperous that King Abimelech requested him to leave. As far as what he travelled, he opened up old wells, however, the local herdsman kept closing the wells up, or dispossessing him from the wells. This might have been such a fearful and challenging experience.

> *Genesis 26:16 (NIV) Then Abimelech said to Isaac, "Move away from us; you have become too powerful for us."*

After a number of dispossessions no one quarrelled over one of the wells which he named Rehoboth. Perseverance and persistence always pays off when we remain obedient to God and trust him in all things. When Isaac eventually moved on to Beersheba, God appeared to him at night and comforted him with a Promise again, but not before first assuring him of His Presence: "***Do not be afraid, for I am with you.***"

> *Genesis 26:22 (NIV) He moved on from there and dug another well, and no one quarrelled over it. He named it Rehoboth, saying, "Now the Lord has given us room and we will flourish in the land."*

> *Genesis 26:23-25 (NIV) [23] From there he went up to Beersheba. [24] That night the LORD appeared to him and said, "I am the God of your father Abraham. **Do not be afraid, for I am with you;** I will bless you and will increase the number of your descendants for the sake of my servant Abraham." [25] Isaac built an altar there and called on the name of the LORD. There he pitched his tent, and **there his servants dug a well.***

Isaac faced famine, fearing for his life as he lived among people who could kill him for his wife, but in the midst of facing all these fearful situations, He followed the directives of the Lord. Many people find themselves in sudden famines. Some live in circumstances where they fear for their own lives. Some fear that they might lose their spouses.

Finding comfort in the directives of God, in the midst of fear, always carry with it a rich reward from the Lord. Isaac overcame his fear by "staying" when God said stay. Him remaining in the land not just kept him but also brought him to a place of abundance.

Moses

When I think of Moses, I think of the many times He faced impossible, fearful situations. **Firstly,** when God called him to go to Pharaoh to let his people go, and then, with all the plagues. **Secondly,** we have the time when they left Egypt and was caught between the Red Sea and the approaching furore of Pharaoh with his descending army. What looked like a certain death situation turned out to be one of the most victorious moments for Israel, but not before Moses faced the mumbling anger of his own people on the one hand, the approaching Egyptian Army, and a Red Sea at the same time. The Bible tells us that it was Moses' faith that brought him through the many fearful circumstances.

> *Hebrews 11:24-29 (NIV) [24] By faith Moses, when he had grown up, refused to be known as the son of Pharaoh's daughter. [25] He chose to be mistreated along with the people of God rather than to enjoy the pleasures of sin for a short time. [26] He regarded disgrace for the sake of Christ as of greater value than the treasures of Egypt, because he was looking ahead to his reward. [27] By faith he left Egypt, not fearing the king's anger; he persevered because he saw him who is invisible. [28] By faith he kept the Passover and the sprinkling of blood, so that the destroyer of the firstborn would not touch the firstborn of Israel. [29] By faith the people passed through the Red Sea as on dry land; but when the Egyptians tried to do so, they were drowned.*

Moses spoke to the Israelites when they were caught between the desert and the Red Sea. His message was clear: "*Do not be _____. Stand firm!*" He even spoke words of hope and trust into them: "*You will see the deliverance the _____ will bring today.*" These were such encouraging words to the hearts of those Israelites, and they continue to encourage many of us today as we face encumbering situations in our lives.

*Exodus 14:13-14 (NIV) [13] Moses answered the people, "**Do not be
afraid. Stand firm and you will see the deliverance the LORD
will bring you today.** The Egyptians you see today you will
never see again. [14] **The LORD will fight for you; you need
only to be still.**"*

When Israel faced their enemies, Moses reminded them, and
comforted them with the Words God spoke to him when they faced
insurmountable situations.

*Deuteronomy 20:1-4 (NIV) [20:1] **When you go to war against
your enemies** and see horses and chariots and **an army greater
than yours, do not be afraid of them,** because the LORD your
God, who brought you up out of Egypt, **will be with you.**
[2] When you are about to go into battle, **the priest shall come
forward and address the army.** [3] He shall say: "Hear, O
Israel, today you are going into battle against your enemies. **Do
not be fainthearted or afraid; do not be terrified or give way to
panic before them.** [4] **For the LORD your God is the one who
goes with you to fight for you against your enemies to give you
victory.**"*

Joshua

The Lord instructed Joshua and the Israelites to not fear as they
prepared themselves to go to possess the promised land.

*Joshua 1:9 (NIV) "Have I not commanded you? Be strong and
courageous. **Do not be terrified; do not be discouraged,** for the
Lord your God will be with you wherever you go."*

Just after Israel got a mighty hiding in a battle with the people of
Ai, the Lord encouraged them again to not fear.

*Joshua 8:1 (NIV) [8:1] Then the LORD said to Joshua, "**Do not be***

*afraid; do not be discouraged. Take the whole army with you
and go up and attack Ai. For I have delivered into your hands
the king of Ai, his people, his city and his land.*

It is easy for us to read these encouragements today, but the same encouragement is given to us as we face our Red seas, our enemies, our dire and challenging circumstances.

David

David once faced a giant, Goliath. One-man instilled fear in an entire army. They feared for their lives. This situation continued for 40 days. The Bible tells us of the extent of the threat and How it impacted them.

> *1 Samuel 17:10-11 (NIV) [10] Then the Philistine said, "**This day I
> defy the ranks of Israel!** Give me a man and let us fight each
> other." [11] **On hearing the Philistine's words, Saul and all the
> Israelites were dismayed and terrified.***

> *1 Samuel 17:16 (NIV) [16] For **forty days** the Philistine came
> forward every morning and evening and took his stand.*

David came to bring refreshments to his brothers, but while he was still speaking to them he heard the thundering voice of Goliath, and saw all the army run from Goliath with great fear.

> *1 Samuel 17:23-24 (NIV) [23] As he was talking with them, Goliath,
> the Philistine champion from Gath, stepped out from his lines
> and shouted his usual defiance, and **David heard it.** [24] **When
> the Israelites saw the man, they all ran from him in great fear.***

David was filled with faith, even though he saw and faced the same enemy. He chose to act in faith and not in fear. He spoke his faith and not his fear.

> *1 Samuel 17:32-36 (NIV) [32] David said to Saul, "Let no one loose heart on account of this Philistine; your servant will go and fight him." [33] Saul replied, "You are not able to go out against this Philistine and fight him; you are only a boy, and he has been a fighting man from his youth." [34] But David said to Saul, "Your servant has been keeping his father's sheep. When a lion or a bear came and carried off a sheep from the flock, [35] I went after it, struck it and rescued the sheep from its mouth. When it turned on me, I seized it by its hair, struck it and killed it. [36] Your servant has killed both the lion and the bear; this uncircumcised Philistine will be like one of them, because he has defied the armies of the living God.*

When fear grips your heart, it brings you down into earthly, faithless speech, however, for David, he rose to the occasion with faith to go and fight this enemy of Israel. His superiors did not think that he had what it took to take on such an experienced warrior, but **David was confident, not in his own strength, but in the God whom he served.** This is such a wonderful example for us who face giants too strong and powerful for us.

> *1 Samuel 17:37 (NIV) [37]* **The LORD who delivered me from the paw of the lion and the paw of the bear will deliver me from the hand of this Philistine."** *Saul said to David,* **"Go, and the LORD be with you."**

David spoke by faith, not in his own strength or ability, but in faith in the living God.

> *1 Samuel 17:45-46 (NIV) [45] David said to the Philistine,* **"You come against me with sword and spear and javelin, but I come against you in the name of the LORD Almighty, the God of the armies of Israel, whom you have defied. [46] This day the LORD will hand you over to me, and I'll strike you down and cut off your head.** *Today I will give the carcasses of the*

*Philistine army to the birds of the air and the beasts of the earth, and **the whole world will know that there is a God in Israel.***

The widow of Zarephath

The widow of Zarephath faced debtors who threatened to take her sons as slaves. When Elijah heard of her plight, he spoke hope into her.

> *1 Kings 17:13 (NIV) [13] Elijah said to her, "**Don't be afraid.** Go home and do as you have said. **But first make a small cake of bread for me from what you have and bring it to me,** and then make something for yourself and your son.*

Once again, we see that the Lord's instruction was to first take an action of faith before she would see God bring tremendous provision. **Obedience and Faith in God is always richly rewarded.** The Bible tells us of How her faith and actions in obedience to the Word of the Lord, was rewarded.

> *1 Kings 17:14-16 (NIV) [14] For this is what the LORD, the God of Israel, says: 'The jar of flour will not be used up and the jug of oil will not run dry until the day the LORD gives rain on the land.'" [15] She went away and did as Elijah had told her. So there was food every day for Elijah and for the woman and her family. [16] For the jar of flour was not used up and the jug of oil did not run dry, in keeping with the word of the LORD spoken by Elijah.*

Isaiah

A prophetic Word came through the prophet Isaiah to encourage us on how to deal with fearful situations.

*Isaiah 41:10-14 (NIV) [10] **So do not fear, for I am with you; do not be dismayed, for I am your God. I will strengthen you and help you; I will uphold you with my righteous right hand.** [11] "All who rage against you will surely be ashamed and disgraced; those who oppose you will be as nothing and perish. [12] **Though you search for your enemies, you will not find them.** Those who wage war against you will be as nothing at all. [13] For I am the LORD, your God, who takes hold of your right hand and says to you, **Do not fear; I will help you.** [14] **Do not be afraid, O worm Jacob, O little Israel, for I myself will help you,"** declares the LORD, your Redeemer, the Holy One of Israel.*

You can live by faith or you can live by fear. Our senses open the doorway to fear or faith. We can look at the same situation through the eyes of fear, or we could look at it with the eyes of faith.

Elisha

The King of Aram was at war with Israel and decided to set up camp against them, however, Elisha sent word to the King of Israel to warn him of the impending ambush and attack. When the King of Aram found out that the man of God foiled his plans by declaring it to the King of Israel, he set out to kill Elisha. During the night the Aramean army surrounded the town where Elisha and his companion was overnighting. Early in the morning when Gehasi woke up, he saw that the whole town was surrounded by this army, and he was afraid. He was fearful, however, when he told the man of God about them being surrounded, the man of God came out and he said: "why are you fearful? Those who are for us, are more than those who are against us." Elisha prayed for his eyes to be opened. When the Lord opened his eyes, he saw the Angels of God, on Chariots of fire, all around them. Gehasi saw that those who were for them were more than those who were against them. They saw the same thing in the natural, however, Elisha also saw in the supernatural, and that made all the difference. May God open our eyes to see, in every situation, that those who are for us are more than those who are against us.

> 2 Kings 6:15-17 (NIV) [15] When the servant of the man of God got up and went out early the next morning, an army with horses and chariots had surrounded the city. **"Oh, my lord, what shall we do?"** the servant asked. [16] **"Don't be afraid,"** the prophet answered. **"Those who are with us are more than those who are with them."** [17] And Elisha prayed, **"O LORD, open his eyes so he may see."** Then the LORD opened the servant's eyes, and he looked and saw the hills full of horses and chariots of fire all around Elisha.

How do we overcome fear?

We overcome fear by faith.

_____ opens the doorway to God's protection, provision and guidance. The Word of God teaches us that we can live by sight or we can live by _____. Fear is often, and mostly, driven by our senses. The more we allow ourselves to be directed through what we see, hear and feel, the more we will fuel the fear in us. However, the more we fuel our decisions by our faith in what God said in His Word, and act accordingly, by faith, we fuel hope and positivity.

> 2 Corinthians 5:7 (KJV) [7] **For we walk by faith, not by sight:**

> 2 Corinthians 4:18 (NIV) [18] **So we fix our eyes not on what is seen, but on what is unseen.** For what is seen is temporary, but what is unseen is eternal.

> 2 Corinthians 4:13 (NIV) [13] It is written: **"I believed; therefore I have spoken." With that same spirit of faith we also believe and therefore speak,**

We overcome fear through our words

We activate the spirit of faith through our words and by focusing our attention on what we see in the spirit rather than what we see in the natural.

Fear is a _____, and we need to take charge of it since we know that **it is** _____ **from God,** and that God did not give us a spirit of fear.

> *2 Timothy 1:7 (KJV) [7] For God hath not given us the **spirit of fear;** but of power, and of love, and of a sound mind.*

Life and death are in the power of our tongues. We need to learn to speak by faith. Speak to your mountain. Speak to your fear. Speak to your circumstances. Speak and declare your faith.

> *Proverbs 18:21 (NIV) [21] **The tongue has the power of life and death,** and those who love it will eat its fruit.*

> *Romans 10:17 (KJV) [17] So then **faith cometh by hearing, and hearing by the word of God.***

> *Mark 11:22-23 (NIV) [22] **"Have faith in God,"** Jesus answered. [23] "I tell you the truth, if anyone says to this mountain, 'Go, throw yourself into the sea,' and does not doubt in his heart but believes that what he says will happen, it will be done for him.***

> *2 Corinthians 4:13 (NIV) [13] It is written: "I believed; therefore I have spoken." With that same spirit of faith we also believe and therefore speak,*

Speak what you _____**, not what you fear.** Faith is speaking what you believe, not what you fear. Activate the spirit of faith by your words, and then act on your faith, not on your fear.

We overcome fear by thinking right.

Our thoughts set a pathway for our faith to follow. **Faith follows your**

_____.

> *Proverbs 23:7 (KJV) [7] For as he thinketh in his heart, so is he: Eat*
> *and drink, saith he to thee; but his heart is not with thee.*

Activate the spirit of faith by your thoughts. Set your mind on things that is above. Setting our thoughts on things that are above us, is to think on the promises of God. It is to think on the goodness and greatness of God.

If we think on the things we fear, they are the things that will come upon us, but if we think on the God who is greater and stronger, and more powerful, then His power will be unlocked over our situation.

> *Job 3:25 (KJV) [25] For the thing which I greatly feared is come*
> *upon me, and that which I was afraid of is come unto me.*

Fear is activated when we give precedence to it in our thoughts, however, the same is true for faith. We need to activate our faith in God in every possible way we can. Activate your faith, over your fears, in your thought dimension, through your words and your actions.

We overcome fear by our faith.

Act by faith and not by what you fear. **We overcome our fears by the profession of our faith.** We overcome fear by acting out our faith in God, His Word and His promises.

> *Hebrews 11:1 (NIV) [11:1] Now faith is being sure of what we hope*
> *for and certain of what we do not see.*

*Hebrews 11:6 (NIV) [6] And **without faith it is impossible to please God, because anyone who comes to him must believe that he exists and that he rewards those who earnestly seek him.***

The men and woman we read about in Chapter 11 were all commended for their faith. In the face of fear, they walked, talked, acted, continued by faith, and that walk by faith was richly rewarded.

There are men and woman going through this session today, and you are facing difficulties, battles, Giants, sickness, debt, storms, and enemies. You might be facing famine and desperate circumstances. The Lord wants me to tell you: "**Don't** _____. **Have** _____ **in God.**"

There are people today who are **in the midst of the storm**, you find that the **enemy already set up camp around you**. The Lord wants me to tell you: "**Don't fear. Have faith in God.**"

I believe we need to pray against that spirit of fear. I believe we need to speak and make faith declarations. I believe we need to set our minds on things above and not below. I believe we need to live by faith and not by sight. Warfare against that spirit of fear according to the Word of God.

Closing declaration

2 Timothy 1:7 For God hath not given us the spirit of fear; but of power, and of love, and of a sound mind.

God has not given me a spirit of fear, but a spirit of _____, power and a sound _____.

Assimilation Sheet for
Fear and Unbelief.

1. Complete the sentence. *Fear and* _____ *are two enemies that can keep us from seeing the fruit of our labour.*

2. What Spirit has God given us according to 2 Timothy 1 verse 7?

_____

_____

3. Complete the sentence. _____ *is that act of embracing one's fears and doubt over against the promises of God.*

4. Complete the sentence. *Fear grips our hearts because we think that God does not* _____ *or* _____ *the desperation of our circumstances.*

5. What is one of the main messages we learn from this account of Hagar? _____

_____

6. Isaac experienced famine, defrauding, many battles with family and enemies who obstructed his work. Give at least two portions of Scriptures of How God helped and encouraged him in dealing with his despondency, fear and unbelief? _____

_____

7. Moses faced many challenges. Name at least two occasions where Moses faced situations that would generally make people succumb to fear and unbelief. _____

_____

_____

8. Moses had two messages for the Israelites. Complete the two sentences. Provide the Scriptural reference as well. *"**Do not be** _____. **Stand firm!**"* He even spoke words of hope and trust into them: *"**You will see the deliverance the** _____ **will bring today.**"*

_____

9. Name any other biblical character we discussed in this session, and what fearful situation they overcame. Provide Scriptural support for your answer. _____

_____

_____

10. Complete the sentence. *We overcome fear by* _____.

11. Complete the sentence. *We overcome fear through our* _____.

12. Provide at least one Scripture to support this strategy of overcoming fear. _____

_____

13. Complete the sentence. **Fear is a** _____, *and we need to take charge of it since we know that* **it is** _____ **from God**, *and that God did not give us a spirit of fear.*

14. Complete the sentence. *We overcome fear by thinking right. Faith follows your* _____.

15. Complete the sentence. *God has not given me a spirit of fear, but a spirit of* _____, *power and a sound* _____.

4

UNFORGIVENESS
SESSION FOUR

Unforgiveness is one of the most devastating things, both for the offended and offender, one can embrace and hold onto. Bad things happen to people of all ages, positions and statuses.

The bad things that happen to us could be **the result of the intentional causing of hurt** or insult, **or of misguided, unintentional causing of hurt and pain.** For most, as victims, we often feel that we were hurt by intention. This felt feeling, experience or encounter of hurt, pain, injustice or rejection triggers within us self-communication which could either be channeled to forgive or to not forgive and excuse the offence. The effects on those who choose to not forgive, especially if it is held onto for an extended period of time, are devastating. We've all been hurt, been offended, been mis-understood, rejected and affected by injustice, however, the way we forgive ultimately determine how we cope with these kinds of challenges today.

This session is not going to be a session to open up every wound or dissect every injustice, however, we will rather attempt to learn ways in which we can more astutely deal with it in a righteous and God-honouring way, by forgiving.

One of the most prominent Teachings of Jesus is on forgiveness. He repeated it on a number of occasions, through a variety of messages, to bring home the power of forgiving others, as well as connecting it to our constant need for forgiveness ourselves. We all desire to be forgiven when we have faulted, but much fewer people are willing to reciprocate such forgiveness where they are wronged. The extent to which we desire to be forgiven is the extent to which we need to understand and apply forgiveness in our lives.

Definition of Forgiveness:

Forgiveness is the renunciation or cessation of _____, indignation or anger as a result of a perceived offence, disagreement, or mistake, or ceasing to demand _____ or restitution.

Forgiveness Balance

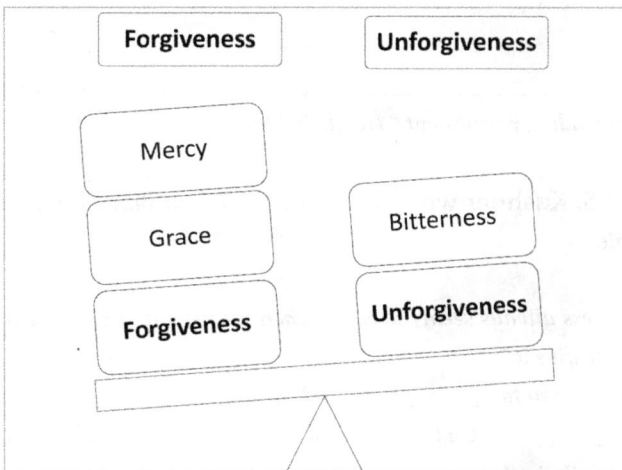

The purpose of this session is to help us outweigh unforgiveness with the weightier effects of forgiveness, grace and mercy.

Jesus is our Example

Jesus is our ultimate example of someone who practiced forgiveness. He set the example when He experienced the ultimate betrayal, hurt, pain, insult, and intentional injustice and still chose to forgive. So, to address unforgiveness, let us explore forgiveness from the WORD OF GOD.

> *Luke 23:34 (NIV) [34] Jesus said, "**Father, forgive them,** for they do not know what they are doing." And they divided up his clothes by casting lots.*

One of the pillars of our Faith is the value we place on _____. FORGIVENESS, alongside LOVE, FAITH, HOLINESS, HUMILITY, FAITHFULNESS, HONESTY, SUBMISSION, OBEDIENCE, COURAGE, COMPASSION, SERVANTHOOD, GENTLENESS, and many more, form the basis of the way we live and ultimately die.

> "_____ *is the ability to pardon an offence without holding resentment." Hendrik J. Vorster*

Harold S. Kushner wrote in his book: ***When Bad Things Happen to Good People;***

> *"Forgiveness always seems so easy, when we need it, and so hard when we need to give it."*
> *"The ability to _____ and the ability to _____ are the _____ God has given us to live fully, bravely, and meaningfully in this less-than-perfect world."*

One of the greatest needs in our day, is the need to be forgiven and be given another chance!

Pandemic Proportions

This need for Forgiveness is so great that it has reached **PANDEMIC** proportions, as it is one of the main reasons for depression, health causes, relationship break-ups, child behavioural disfunction and many more of societies challenges.

God, in His Graciousness and Compassion made eternal provision to meet our need for forgiveness.

Defining Forgiveness

There are primarily two GREEK words for forgiveness and describing its meaning:

- **Aphiemi** - means to: send away, leave alone, or *"To abandon."*

- **Charizomai** - means to: show favor, give freely, graciously forgave, forgive.

The Basis for giving and receiving Forgiveness is found in God. Today we will explore the Biblical requirements for Forgiveness. We will also look at the provision for forgiveness by Christ, and His message to each one of us today.

THE BASIS OF FORGIVENESS IS FOUND IN GOD.

God is a God of Forgiveness. Throughout the Bible we read that God is a "Forgiving God."

> *Numbers 14:18 (NIV) [18] 'The LORD is slow to anger, abounding in love and **forgiving sin** and rebellion. Yet he does not leave the guilty unpunished; he punishes the children for the sin of the fathers to the third and fourth generation.'*

*Daniel 9:9 (NIV) [9] **The Lord our God is merciful and forgiving,** even though we have rebelled against him;*

*Nehemiah 9:17 (NIV) [17] They refused to listen and failed to remember the miracles you performed among them. They became stiff-necked and, in their rebellion, appointed a leader in order to return to their slavery. **But you are a forgiving God, gracious and compassionate, slow to anger and abounding in love.** Therefore, you did not desert them,*

The Nature of God is that He is a Forgiving God, Gracious and Compassionate. The Psalmists remind us of this truth.

*Psalms 86:5 (NIV) [5] **You are forgiving and good, O Lord,** abounding in love to all who call to you.*

*Psalms 130:4 (NIV) [4] **But with you there is forgiveness; therefore, you are feared.***

There is Forgiveness with God.

The God we serve is a forgiving God. Any pursuit of Him will find Him to be the most forgiving, understanding and compassionate God we hope to have dealing with our shortcomings, faults, mistakes, intentional and unintentional sins.

THE BIBLICAL REQUIREMENTS FOR FORGIVENESS.

When God gave the law to Moses, He also gave instructions for sacrifices to be made for the redemption and forgiveness of sins. The sacrifice had to be consistent with the offence for which pardon was sought. The "bigger the sin," the larger the sacrifice that was required.

*Leviticus 4:19-20 (NIV) [19] **He shall remove all the fat from it and burn it on the altar, [20] and do with this bull just as***

he did with the bull for the sin offering. In this way the
priest will make atonement for them, and they will be
forgiven.

A. The offering of sacrifices is the first part of seeking Forgiveness.

According to the transgression, the sinner brought sin offerings under the Old Testament law. So, when you sinned, and wanted to be pardoned for your sin, you will bring to the priest a sacrifice to be offered, to be killed, to give its life, as a sin offering for your sin. The Priest will slaughter the dove, lamb or bull, after hearing your confession, and then pardon you. The sacrifice will pay for your sins and you will be free from the guilt and punishment. It was the blood that was shed that satisfied the requirements of God to forgive and pardon sinners. The Bible teaches that *"without the shedding of blood there is no forgiveness."*

> *Hebrews 9:22 In fact, the law requires that nearly everything be*
> *cleansed with blood, and **without the shedding of blood there is***
> ***no forgiveness.***

For us as New Testament Believers, we are blessed since Christ became our Sacrificial Lamb who took away the sins of the world and paid for our sins by shedding _____ and being our Atoning Sacrifice.

> *Ephesians 1:7 In him **we have redemption through his blood, the***
> ***forgiveness of sins,** in accordance with the riches of God's grace*

> *Hebrews 9:13-14 The blood of goats and bulls and the ashes of a*
> *heifer sprinkled on those who are ceremonially unclean **sanctify***
> ***them so that they are outwardly clean.** 14 **How much more,***
> ***then, will the blood of Christ,** who through the eternal Spirit*
> *offered himself unblemished to God, **cleanse our consciences***

from acts that lead to death, so that we may serve the living God!

B. The second part of this redemptive process was that, the sacrifice, or offering, had to be acceptable to God, before forgiveness was given.

Right from when the very first offerings were brought to God by Cain and Abel, we see that one was accepted, and the other not. When Adam and Eve sinned in the Garden, the covering God made to cover the sin and shame, was made of skin. An animal lost its life to cover the sin of Adam and Eve.

Only the death of a sacrificial animal could appease the Father for the sins committed. This action of the Father set in motion a principle for what was acceptable to pardon sin; it was the shedding of blood that would bring a covering and pardon for sin. The sacrifice needed to be _____. No deformed, cripple or blemished sacrifice would suffice.

> *Genesis 3:21 The **Lord God made garments of skin** for Adam and his wife and clothed them.*

> *Genesis 4:4 But Abel brought fat portions from some of the firstborn of his flock. **The Lord looked with favor on Abel and his offering**, 5 but on Cain and his offering he did not look with favor. So, Cain was very angry, and his face was downcast.*

> *Leviticus 1:3-4 "'If the offering is a burnt offering from the herd, he is to offer a male without defect. He must present it at the entrance to the Tent of Meeting so that **it will be acceptable to the Lord**. 4 He is to lay his hand on the head of the burnt offering, and it will be accepted on his behalf to make atonement for him."*

It was essential to bring sacrifices that would be acceptable to

God, in order to receive forgiveness of sins. When Christ became our Sacrificial Lamb, His sacrifice was accepted. We see in Romans that: *"God presented Jesus as a sacrifice of atonement."* In the Words of John: *"God so loved the world that He gave His One and Only Son."* This level and kind of giving, of a Redeemer, is beyond our reason or understanding. God truly loves us.

> *Romans 3:25 **God presented him as a sacrifice of atonement,** through faith in his blood. He did this to demonstrate his justice, because in his forbearance he had left the sins committed beforehand unpunished—*

> *1 John 2:2 **He is the atoning sacrifice for our sins,** and not only for ours but also for the sins of the whole world.*

> *John 1:29 The next day John saw Jesus coming toward him and said, "Look, **the Lamb of God, who takes away the sin of the world!***

_____ became our Sacrificial Lamb, who took away our sins. It is through Christ meeting the requirements to pay the price for our sins, that forgiveness is offered to all who believe in Him and trust in Him for their Forgiveness. If the blood of animals brought pardon to the offenders, how much more did the Blood of Christ accomplish forgiveness to those who confess, repent and believe in His Gracious Pardon.

It is so true what the Word tells us in Hebrews: *"**How much more, then, will the blood of Christ cleanse our consciences from acts that lead to death.**"* Christ sacrifice, and offering His Blood, cleanses us from all sin and unrighteousness.

> *Hebrews 9:13-14 The blood of goats and bulls and the ashes of a heifer sprinkled on those who are ceremonially unclean **sanctify them so that they are outwardly clean. 14 How much more, then, will the blood of Christ,** who through the eternal Spirit*

*offered himself unblemished to God, **cleanse our consciences
from acts that lead to death,** so that we may serve the
living God!*

*1 Peter 1:18-19 For you know that it was not with perishable things
such as silver or gold that **you were redeemed** from the empty
way of life handed down to you from your forefathers, 19 but
with the precious blood of Christ, a lamb without blemish or
defect.*

We have been redeemed by the Blood that Jesus Christ shed. He
paid the price for our sins. Through His sacrifice and the shedding of
His Blood we have forgiveness of our sins.

This forgiveness is extended to all who _____. This
forgiveness covers all sin. This forgiveness is for everyone.

C. The Third part is for us to accept His Forgiveness.

We need to accept His forgiveness. The New Testament proclaimed
the same message that: *"**without the shedding of blood there is no
forgiveness.**"* Conversely, with the Blood of Christ there is Forgiveness.
Christ shed His blood for your and my sins. We are forgiven because
of His great sacrifice.

If God accepted Christ's sacrifice and His blood offered for the
remission of our sins, then **we ought to accept His sacrifice and
forgiveness of our sins** as well. There is a direct connection between
the shedding of Christ's Blood and our forgiveness.

*Hebrews 9:22 (NIV) [22] In fact, the law requires that nearly
everything be cleansed with blood, and **without the shedding of
blood there is no forgiveness.***

*Hebrews 9:12 (NIV) [12] He did not enter by means of the blood of
goats and calves; but he entered the Most Holy Place once for all
by his own blood, having **obtained eternal redemption.***

Colossians 2:13 (NIV) [13] When you were dead in your sins and in
the uncircumcision of your sinful nature, God made you alive
*with Christ. **He forgave us all our sins,***

Acts 10:43 (NIV)
*[43] All the prophets testify about him that **everyone who believes***
in him receives forgiveness of sins through his name."

Every time we partake of the Lord's Table we celebrate and accept
His forgiveness of our sins.

*Matthew 26:28 (NIV) [28] **This is my blood** of the covenant, which*
*is poured out for many **for the forgiveness of sins.***

We all thank God for His Grace and Mercy to forgive us of our
sins, however, there is an extremely important aspect to receiving this
forgiveness that, if missed or not applied, might leave you in the same
misery as if you never confessed your sin and sought forgiveness, and
that is that God requires us to extend forgiveness to those who
"sinned" against us.

God's Forgiveness is conditional.

Christ offers us unreserved forgiveness, but **there is a condition**
attached to it: **we need to also forgive.** Jesus taught us in the "Our
Father" prayer, to *"forgive us our sins as we forgive those who have*
sinned against us."

*Matthew 6:12-15 (NIV) "[12] **Forgive us our debts, as we also have***
***forgiven our debtors.** [13] And lead us not into temptation but*
*deliver us from the evil one.' [14] **For if you forgive men when***
they sin against you, your heavenly Father will also forgive
you.** [15] **But if you do not forgive men their sins, your Father
will not forgive your sins."

Forgiving others is as important to God as receiving forgiveness from Him for our sins. Jesus told a number of Parables to emphasise the importance of forgiveness. Jesus reminds us of the practice of forgiveness through parables. In two parables Jesus points us to forgive like God and not like man.

The unmerciful servant.

Jesus precedes this Parable by teaching the principle of forgiveness.

> *Matthew 18:21-22 The Parable of the Unmerciful Servant "Then Peter came to Jesus and asked, 'Lord, how many times shall I forgive my brother when he sins against me? Up to seven times?' 22 Jesus answered, 'I tell you, not seven times, but seventy-seven times.'"*

In this Parable Jesus taught that the Kingdom of Heaven is like a Master who wanted to settle accounts, or the debts, that his servants had with Him. When one of the servants was brought to Him because of his Large debt, into the millions in today's terms, he begged for mercy when his Master wanted to have him and his whole family, including all he owned, sold to cover the debts. His Master took pity on him and forgave him his debt and let him go debt-free. However, as that pardoned servant went out, he saw another servant who owed him only a few dollars, but instead of pardoning him, he put him in prison until his debt was paid. When the Master heard of this ungrateful and inconsistent behaviour of someone whom he pardoned of so much, he called him to account because of his unmerciful behaviour.

> *Matthew 18:32-35 "Then the master called the servant in. 'You wicked servant,' he said, 'I cancelled all that debt of yours because you begged me to. 33 Shouldn't you have had mercy on your fellow servant just as I had on you?' 34 In anger his master turned him over to the jailers to be tortured, until he*

should pay back all he owed. 35 'This is how my heavenly
Father will treat each of you unless you forgive your brother
from your heart.'''

This parable epitomises our response in many respects; we plead our case for forgiveness daily for the things in which we transgressed, yet at the same time, almost without consideration, refuses to engage the thought of leniency, grace, pardon or forgiveness towards those who offended, hurt or transgressed towards us.

Although we could see it clearly explained and understood in this parable, we often fail to connect this parable to the realities of our actions and how we practice forgiveness. The concluding words of the Lord Jesus should serve as a stern warning and reminder that our **"Heavenly Father will treat each one of us"** with the same measure, unless we *"forgive our brother from our heart."*

This conversation would not be complete if we did not revisit the "yardstick" or **"Rule of Thumb"** for practicing forgiveness: **"I tell you, not seven times, but seventy-seven times."**

The Millstone

The teaching of Jesus on Sin and the Millstone serves as another reminder to watch ourselves, that we do not cause others to sin, but also to live with a certain preparedness to forgive those who "sin" against us without reservation. Here again we learn the same principle on forgiveness: *"If your brother sins, rebuke him, and if he repents, forgive him. If he sins against you seven times in a day, and seven times comes back to you and says, 'I repent,' forgive him."*

> *Luke 17:1-4 Jesus said to his disciples: "Things that cause people to*
> *sin are bound to come, but woe to that person through whom*
> *they come. It would be better for him to be thrown into the sea*
> *with a millstone tied around his neck than for him to cause one*
> *of these little ones to sin. So, watch yourselves. If your brother*
> *sins, rebuke him, and **if he repents, forgive him**. If he sins*

against you seven times in a day, and seven times comes back to you and says, 'I repent,' forgive him."

Someone has said, *"We are never more like God than when we can forgive others."*

Let us take a few moments to explore this connection between receiving forgiveness for our sins and the forgiveness we are willing to offer to others. Throughout the Scriptures we are taught four basic principles of forgiveness.

Principle 1: God Forgives sins.

*Matthew 6:12-13 (NIV) [12] **Forgive us our debts**, as we also have forgiven our debtors. [13] And lead us not into temptation but deliver us from the evil one.'*

The first principle is that **God is the Author of Forgiveness**. He desires to be Merciful to all who seek forgiveness from Him for their sins. The reason for us praying: *"**Forgive us our sins**"* is rooted in the deepest desire of man to live without guilt, rejection or guilt, and an acknowledgment that true forgiveness is only found in Him.

*Mark 2:7 "Why does this fellow talk like that? He's blaspheming! **Who can forgive sins but God alone?"***

Many times, people struggle with unforgiveness since they fail to accept the forgiveness of the Father, even after repeated offerings of repentance. Settle this today: *His Forgiveness stands secure for all who confess and repent of their sins.*

Principle 2: Forgive Those Who Sin Against you.

Matthew 6:12(NLT) "And forgive us our sins, just as we have forgiven those who have sinned against us."

Matthew 18:21 – Then Peter came to Him and said, "Lord, how often shall my brother sin against me, and I forgive him? Up to seven times?"

To forgive completely requires one of the most difficult of all adjustments, but Jesus describes it so simply: ***"Just as we need forgiveness, so we must forgive others."***

Principle 3: Forgive and be forgiven

If we forgive, God will _____ us.

*Matthew 6:14 "For if you forgive men their trespasses, **your heavenly Father will also forgive you.**"*

*Luke 6:37 "Judge not, and you shall not be judged. Condemn not, and you shall not be condemned. Forgive, **and you will be forgiven.**"*

It all depends on us. As we forgive, we will be forgiven. As we show mercy, mercy shall be shown to us.

"We need not climb up into heaven to see whether our sins are forgiven. Let us look into our hearts and see if we can forgive others."
- Thomas Watson

Principle 4: If we do not Forgive, we will not be forgiven.

Jesus gave this warning about forgiveness: If we refuse to forgive others, God will also refuse to forgive us.

*Matthew 6:15 (NIV) "[15] **But if you do not forgive men their sins, your Father will not forgive your sins.**"*

Mark 11:25 And when you stand praying, if you hold anything against anyone, forgive him, so that your Father in heaven may forgive you your sins."'

This is the reality check on holding on to unforgiveness. If we hold back, or refuse to forgive men their trespasses against us, then our Heavenly Father will also refuse to forgive us our sins. We are warned against the sin of an unforgiving heart, which often results in a bitter spirit that robs us of the blessings God reserved for us.

Hebrews 12:15 (NIV) [15] See to it that no one misses the grace of God and that no bitter root grows up to cause trouble and defile many.

In one sense refusing to forgive others reveals a lack of appreciation for the mercy received from God.

AFTERWORD

As Followers of Jesus Christ **we clothe ourselves with the forbearance** to be merciful and to forgive whatever grievances we may have with others.

Ephesians 4:32 Be kind and compassionate to one another, forgiving each other, just as in Christ God forgave you.

Colossians 3:12-13 Therefore, as God's chosen people, holy and dearly loved, clothe yourselves with compassion, kindness, humility, gentleness and patience. 13 Bear with each other and forgive whatever grievances you may have against one another. Forgive as the Lord forgave you.

Almost nothing shows the love we have for one another, as does the way we are merciful, forgiving and forbearing with others.

Biblical Examples

Every believer should seek to practice the forgiving spirit of these examples:

Joseph

Joseph endured unjust treatment and the ultimate betrayal from his family, by being sold as a slave into a foreign nation. His brothers essentially ensured that he was as good as dead when they sold him. Joseph endured false accusation from Potiphar's wife, which landed him in prison. His companions in prison also let him down by not keeping their word. He almost endured a lifetime of betrayal, false accusation and rejection, yet he forgave his perpetrators.

> *Genesis 50:19-21 (NIV) [19] But Joseph said to them, "Don't be afraid. Am I in the place of God? [20] You intended to harm me, but God intended it for good to accomplish what is now being done, the saving of many lives. [21] So then, don't be afraid. I will provide for you and your children." And he reassured them and spoke kindly to them.*

His kindness not only extended to forgiving and pardoning them, he also provided for them and their families. Many people live the proverbial "*Joseph's Life*," they have been betrayed, been rejected and experienced false accusations levelled against them. Like Joseph found it in his heart to forgive those who subjected him a life-time of abuse and living a degenerated life, we too should forgive those who intentionally and purposefully hurt and abused us.

Stephen

Stephen was this powerful witness for Jesus Christ who, in the midst of preaching and defending the faith, was stoned to death. He did not defend himself against his assaulters, or retaliated with threats and accusations, but chose to continue to testify and to pray for his oppressors that God would forgive them and not hold their sin against them. What an example of the ultimate test to practice forgiveness. Stephen did it: He forgave those who stoned him to death for preaching and testifying for Jesus Christ.

> Acts 7:60 (NIV) [60] Then he fell on his knees and cried out, "Lord, do not hold this sin against them." When he had said this, he fell asleep.

As principle-centered people, we are called upon again and again to forgive. The principles of forgiveness are given priority throughout the scriptures to be placed into practice.

Jesus

Jesus modelled forgiveness to us, even when He faced the most challenging of circumstances. Sometimes we think that: "*if I was just in a better headspace,*" or "*if I wasn't in so much pain and discomfort, then I would possibly more easily forgive,*" however, Christ set us an example to follow.

> Luke 23:34 (NIV) [34] Jesus said, "Father, forgive them, for they do not know what they are doing." And they divided up his clothes by casting lots.

Jesus remains our ultimate example of someone who endured the harshest of unjust treatments any human ever endured, yet chose to forgive.

Communion

It is through our participation of communion that we affirm the forgiveness of our sins. Every time we take the cup, we partake of the Blood of Jesus Christ. His Blood washes and cleanses us from all sin and shame. One of the sure-fast ways we deal with unforgiveness is by consciously partaking of the blood of Jesus. When we take the cup, after examining ourselves, we both pardon others of their offences against us, and we receive and accept our forgiveness and pardon from the Lord.

> *Matthew 26:28 (NIV) [28] This is my blood of the covenant, which is poured out for many for the forgiveness of sins.*

How do we deal with unforgiveness?

- Affirm Almighty God as the Forgiver of sin.
- Affirm that He made significant and complete provision for the remission of all the sins of the world, including yours.
- Take time to consider all the people who committed offences against you and forgive them. Once you truly forgiven them, and asked God to forgive them and to pardon them, then address your own needs for forgiveness.
- Confess your sins and ask God to forgive you.
- Affirm that you seek and accept His Forgiveness for all your sins.

Assimilation Sheet for
Unforgiveness.

1. Complete the sentence. *One of the most prominent Teachings of Jesus is on* _____.

2. Complete the definition of Forgiveness. *Forgiveness is the renunciation or cessation of* _____, *indignation or anger as a result of a perceived offence, disagreement, or mistake, or ceasing to demand* _____ *or restitution.*

3. Complete the sentence. *The ability to* _____ *and the ability to* _____ *are the weapons God has given us to live fully, bravely, and meaningfully in this less-than-perfect world.*

4. Which Scriptures teach that God is a forgiving God?

_____

_____

5. Provide Scriptural proof that: *"without the shedding of blood there is no forgiveness."* _____

_____

6. Provide Scriptural proof that: "Jesus is the Lamb of God."

_____

_____

7. Jesus taught about a condition upon which God will forgive us of our sins. What is that condition for us to receive our forgiveness? Provide Scriptures. _____

_____

_____

8. We looked at Four Principles of Forgiveness. Name the Four and provide at least one Scripture for each.

Principle 1: _____

Principle 2: _____

Principle 3: _____

Principle 4: _____

9. Complete the sentence. *As Followers of Jesus Christ* **we** _____ **ourselves with the forbearance** *to be merciful and to forgive whatever grievances we may have with others.*

5

LUST OF THE FLESH AND THE LUST OF THE EYES

SESSION FIVE

> *1 John 2:15-17 Do not love the world or anything in the world. If anyone loves the world, the love of the Father is not in him. 16 For everything in the world—the cravings of sinful man, the lust of his eyes and the boasting of what he has and does— comes not from the Father but from the world. 17 The world and its desires pass away, but the man who does the will of God lives forever.*

L ust is a terrible **evil** _____ in many people's lives. It manifests itself in numerous ways. Most will deny its existence in them until the Holy Spirit's conviction unlayer the masks behind which they hide to attempt to disguise it.

When Jesus taught us through the Parable of the Sower, He emphasised how the thistles and thorns would choke the seed and make it unfruitful.

To choke something means that you block its breathing capacity and enforcing a cruel destructive death.

This is exactly what lust does in one's life; it deprives the good seed in you to remain alive. It essentially kills it and makes all the good potential to be eliminated and to be made unfruitful.

> *Mark 4:18-19 "Still others, like seed sown among thorns, hear the word; 19 but the worries of this life, the deceitfulness of wealth and **the desires for other things come in and** _____ **the word, making it** _____ "*

> *Luke 8:13-14 "Those on the rock are the ones who receive the word with joy when they hear it, but they have no root. They believe for a while, but in the time of testing they fall away. 14 The seed that fell among thorns stands for those who hear, but as they go on their way **they are choked by** life's worries, riches and pleasures, and **they do not** _____."*

It is this "***desire***" for other things and for "***pleasures***" that choke the good seed of the Word in our lives and ultimately make us unfruitful and keep us from maturing in our faith. Nowadays you can't watch regular television without being bombarded with "pleasures." It is the encompassing extent and result of these "pleasures" that is not openly disclosed.

The Bible teaches us, both what these acts are, which responds to the sinful nature, as well as the outcome for those who persist in such acts. May the Lord grant us a soberness to assess ourselves in the light of Scripture.

Galatians chapter 5 unpacks those acts of the sinful nature that ultimately "choke" us and lead us to a place where we will miss out on inheriting the Kingdom of God.

> *Galatians 5:19-21 "The acts of the sinful nature are obvious: sexual immorality, impurity and debauchery; idolatry and witchcraft; hatred, discord, jealousy, fits of rage, selfish ambition, dissensions, factions and envy; drunkenness, orgies, and the like. **I warn you, as I did before, that those who live like this will not inherit the kingdom of God."***

When we allow ourselves to lured by *"the lust of our _____,"* or *"the lust of the _____"* then we find these very things present: *"sexual immorality, impurity and debauchery; idolatry and witchcraft; hatred, discord, jealousy, fits of rage, selfish ambition, dissensions, factions and envy; drunkenness, orgies, and the like."*

These Scriptures do not address those who still live under the blindfold of their old nature, no, these Scriptures address those in the Church. These Scriptures exhorts us to address these carnal aptitudes in a deep yieldedness to the sanctification work of the Holy Spirit. It is not to spoil our fun or to deprive us from living with a sense of gratification, but to bring us to a place of true, and lasting fulfilment.

> *Romans 13:14 Rather,* **clothe yourselves** *with the Lord Jesus Christ, and* **do not think about how to gratify the _____** *of the* **sinful nature.**

It seems from this Scripture that it is essential that we make a concerted effort to rather please the Holy Spirit's desires inside of us, rather than the unsatisfiable promptings of the flesh. The outcome of continuing to live for the gratifications of the flesh will leave you empty, unsatisfied and unfulfilled. They will also deprive you of seeing the seed of your efforts bearing lasting fruit.

> *Galatians 5:16-17 So, I say, live by the Spirit, and you will not gratify the desires of the sinful nature. For the sinful nature desires what is contrary to the Spirit, and the Spirit what is contrary to the sinful nature. They are in conflict with each other, so that you do not do what you want.*

> *Galatians 5:24 Those who belong to Christ Jesus have crucified the sinful nature with its passions and desires.*

> *Ephesians 2:3 All of us also lived among them at one time,* **gratifying the cravings of our sinful nature and following its**

desires and thoughts. Like the rest, we were by nature objects of wrath.

It is this, succumbing to the gratifications of the flesh that will keep you from seeing fruit on your labour in the Lord. When we sow to please the Holy Spirit, we will reap eternal benefits, however, if we continue to sow to satisfy the gratifications of the flesh, it will only bring forth a harvest of sin.

How do we crucify the lust of the flesh?

Fast and Pray.

Nothing breaks the back of fleshly desires as does fasting and prayer. Jesus ones said that: *"this kind does not come out expect by fasting and prayer."* This remains true for every Believer. When we submit ourselves to a time of Fasting and prayer, we actively crucify the lust and desires of the flesh.

> Mark 9:29 (NIV) 29 He replied, "This kind can come out only by prayer and fasting."

In the well-known chapter on Fasting, Isaiah outlines the very things we need to crucify in our lives through fasting.

> Isaiah 58:6-9 (NIV) 6 "Is not this the kind of fasting I have chosen: to loose the chains of injustice and untie the cords of the yoke, to set the oppressed free and break every yoke? 7 Is it not to share your food with the hungry and to provide the poor wanderer with shelter — when you see the naked, to clothe them, and not to turn away from your own flesh and blood? 8 Then your light will break forth like the dawn, and your healing will quickly appear; then your righteousness will go before you, and the glory of the LORD will be your rear guard. 9 Then you will call, and

the LORD will answer; you will cry for help, and he will say: Here am I.

Take a 21-day Spiritual food challenge.

Take a _____ Spiritual Food challenge. The purpose of this is simply to fill yourself with more of God as we believe that God will set you free from the spirit of lust this weekend. Jesus' warning in Luke chapter eleven compels us to take this action to ensure that we replace every area lust occupied and fill it with the Word and the Holy Spirit.

> Luke 11:24-26 (AMP) 24 When the unclean spirit has gone out of a person, it roams through waterless places in search [of a place] of rest (release, refreshment, ease); and finding none it says, I will go back to my house from which I came.
> 25 And when it arrives, it finds [the place] swept and put in order and furnished and decorated.
> 26 And it goes and brings other spirits, seven [of them], more evil than itself, and they enter in, settle down, and dwell there; and the last state of that person is worse than the first.

Take 21 days to only feed yourself with the Word of God, before taking any physical food. Read and pray through 21 New Testament Books, starting with Revelation. Some days will take you 90 minutes, but others just a few short minutes, however, take the time to ask the Holy Spirit to help you and lead you out of lust. How we feed and fill our mind with the Word of God, will help us overcome whatever is tormenting and enslaving us.

Confess your deliverance.

Make confessions of what you are trusting God to accomplish in your life. We overcome the evil one by applying the _____ of Jesus and by the _____ of our mouths.

> *Revelation 12:11* **They overcame him by the _____ of**
> **the Lamb and by the _____ of their testimony;**
> *they did not love their lives so much as to shrink from death.*

Get an accountability partner.

The Bible teaches that we should confess our sins _____ so that we may be healed. Being free from lust will bring healing to your life. Many times, when people confess their sins, especially to those counted as elders, they help us by holding us _____. Their prayers have tremendous power and are effective in seeing us free and delivered.

> *James 5:16 Therefore,* **confess your sins to each other** *and pray for*
> *each other so that you may be healed. The prayer of a righteous*
> *man is powerful and effective.*

Be filled, and remain filled, with the Spirit.

Nothing is as sure a guard against the enemy's assaults as remaining filled with the Holy Spirit. The more we remain filled with the Holy Spirit, the more we will find ourselves suppressing the evil desires of the flesh. Remember, the flesh and the spirit are in competition and opposition to each other. The one you feed and give pre-eminence to, is the one who will reign and bear fruit in your life.

> *Galatians 5:16-17 Life by the Spirit "So, I say, live by the*
> _____, *and you will not gratify the* _____
> *of the sinful nature. 17 For the sinful nature desires what is*

contrary to the Spirit, and the Spirit what is contrary to the sinful nature. They are in conflict with each other, so that you do not do what you want."

Galatians 5:24-25 *"Those who belong to Christ Jesus have crucified the sinful nature with its passions and desires. 25 Since we live by the Spirit, let us keep in step with the Spirit."*

I pray that you will find true freedom in Christ Jesus. The next part is dedicated to maintaining the freedom Christ brought into our lives.

Assimilation Sheet for
The Lust of the Flesh and the Lust of the Eyes.

1. Complete the sentence. *Lust is a terrible evil _____ in many people's lives.*

2. Which things are not from the Father according to 1 John 2 verses 15 to 17? _____

_____

3. What two things does the thorns do in our lives, according to Mark chapter 4 verses 18 to 19. _____

_____

4. Write down those things that are described in Galatians chapter 5 as "acts of the sinful nature." _____

_____

_____

_____

5. Write down the five things we can do to deal with Lust in our lives. _____

_____

_____

6. Give one Scriptures to substantiate the first two approached of dealing with Lust. _____

7. Complete the sentence. *We overcome the evil one by applying the _____ of Jesus and by the _____ of our mouths.*

8. Why is it important to confess your sins, one to another? What Scripture do you base this belief on? _____

_____

9. Complete the sentence. *"Live by the _____, and you will not gratify the _____ of the sinful nature."*

6

FAITH AND OBEDIENCE
SESSION SIX

Luke 11:24-26 "When an evil spirit comes out of a man, it goes through arid places seeking rest and does not find it. Then it says, 'I will return to the house I left.' 25 When it arrives, it finds the house swept clean and put in order. 26 Then it goes and takes seven other spirits more wicked than itself, and they go in and live there. And the final condition of that man is worse than the first."

The last thing any of us want is to see all the good work God accomplished in your life, this weekend, become undone in weeks to come.

- *How do we remain free and delivered?*
- *How do we retain the good measure God poured out into our lives this weekend?*

Our **first defence** is to stay in a place of being full of the _____. Our **second defence** is to _____ with those who will encourage and spur us on in this journey with

Christ. Our **third defence** is to stay in the _____ and _____ together with fellow Believers as often as what we are able.

I believe that we will do well to head to the advice and action steps we've taken throughout this weekend to decisively deal with the affected areas of our lives, however, there is another aspect that requires our attention, and that is the _____ **to obey**. Hebrews chapter 4 recounts the reasons why a generation of Israelites did not enter into the land promised to them, as well as why only 2 people, out of an entire generation, entered into the Promised land.

Many people experience deliverance from the power of slavery, but only a few take possession of the promised land God set before them. I pray that you will set your heart on the Promises God set before you, and consciously turn your back on the Egypt – place of slavery — and by faith take possession of the land occupied by giants.

Faith to Obey.

> *Hebrews 4:1-2 NIV "Therefore, since the promise of entering his rest still stands, let us be careful that none of you be found to have fallen short of it. For we also have had the good news proclaimed to us, just as they did; but **the message they heard was of no value to them**, because **they did not share the faith of those who obeyed**."*

In this session I want to speak about *Faith to* _____. One morning, whilst reading the Word of God, the Lord spoke to me through His Word. Allow me to share this thought with you.

> *Hebrews 4:2 (NIV) "For we also have had the good news proclaimed to us, just as they did; but the message they heard was of no value to them, **because they did not share the faith of those who obeyed**."*

The latter part of this verse spoke to me: **"the faith of those who obeyed."** The Word of God is powerful and is full of benefits, however these benefits are reserved for those who **combine their** _____ **with obedience.**

An entire nation received a promise of a Promised Land; however, it was only Joshua and Caleb who entered that Promised Land. **Their Promised land was connected to their faith to obey.** The Amplified Bible states it beautifully:

> *Hebrews 4:2 (AMP) [2] For indeed we have had the glad tidings [Gospel of God] proclaimed to us just as truly as they [the Israelites of old did when the good news of deliverance from bondage came to them]; but the message they heard did not benefit them, because it was not mixed with faith (with *the leaning of the entire personality on God in absolute trust and confidence in His power, wisdom, and goodness) by those who heard it; *neither were they united in faith with the ones [Joshua and Caleb] who heard (did believe).*

I was thinking about the Faith of a Joshua and Caleb. They were remarkable men. They were part of the 12 spies, whom Moses selected to go and spy out the Promised land. Only Joshua and Caleb came back believing that they could conquer and possess the Promised land. _____ *out of twelve* became two out of an entire nation. 12 Spies went out, 10 came back with a negative report, a report of unbelief, a report of impossibility, a report of fear and of rebellion, and two came back with a report of Hope, Faith, Obedience, and possibility. The Bible says that the twelve reported and confirmed that it was a "land flowing with milk and honey," but the main emphasis of ten of them was on the impossibilities of conquering the powerful possessors of the land.

> *Numbers 13:27-28 (NIV) [27] They gave Moses this account: "We went into the land to which you sent us, and it does flow with milk and honey! Here is its fruit. [28] **But the people who live***

there are powerful, and the cities are fortified and very large. We even saw descendants of Anak there."

Among the same 12 spies was Joshua and Caleb, who silenced the revolting people, and said that they *"should go up and take possession of the land."*

Numbers 13:30 (NIV) Then Caleb silenced the people before Moses and said, "We should go up and take possession of the land, for we can certainly do it."

Caleb and Joshua found themselves among unbelievers who did not believe that the God who miraculously delivered them from the hands of the mighty Pharaoh could give them a land that He promised to them. 10 of the 12 spies kept on discouraging the Israelites to the extent that the Israelites were filled with fear and unbelief.

Numbers 13:31-33 (NIV) [31] But the men who had gone up with him said, "We can't attack those people; they are stronger than we are." [32] And they spread among the Israelites a bad report about the land they had explored. They said, "The land we explored devours those living in it. All the people we saw there are of great size. [33] We saw the Nephilim there (the descendants of Anak come from the Nephilim). We seemed like grasshoppers in our own eyes, and we looked the same to them."

This back and forth struggle went on. It will be the same in your and my Christian walk, many will continue to echo the impossibilities. Many might say to you that the Promises of God has impossible conditions attached to them. Many might say that you will not be able to accomplish what was impossible for past generations. Many might say that you should simply settle for "your lot." There are not many Joshua's and Caleb's, who resolve to heed to the voice of faith inside of them and trust in the God who is able to make the impossible possible.

> *Numbers 14:6-9 (NIV) [6] **Joshua** son of Nun and **Caleb** son of Jephunneh, who were among those who had explored the land, **tore their clothes [7] and said to the entire Israelite** assembly, **"The land we passed through and explored is exceedingly good. [8]** If the LORD is pleased with us, **he will lead us into that land**, a land flowing with milk and honey, and **will give it to us. [9] Only do not rebel against the LORD**. And **do not be afraid** of the people of the land, **because we will swallow them up. Their protection is gone, but the LORD is with us. Do not be afraid of them."*

Finally, the Lord expressed His dismay with the people's response of rebellion and fear. Was it not for **Moses** who **interceded** before the Lord for the people, the whole nation would have been wiped out. May Father find in us a "Moses" who would stand in the gap on behalf of our Nation, City, Family and even church, to pray for their unbelief to be replaced with faith and obedience.

> *Numbers 14:20-24 (NIV) "[20] The LORD replied, "I have forgiven them, as you asked. [21] Nevertheless, as surely as I live and as surely as the glory of the LORD fills the whole earth, [22] not one of the men who saw my glory and the miraculous signs I performed in Egypt and in the desert but **who disobeyed me** and **tested me ten times**— [23] not one of them will ever see the land I promised on oath to their forefathers. No one who has treated me with contempt will ever see it. [24] But because my servant Caleb has a different spirit and follows me wholeheartedly, I will bring him into the land he went to, and his descendants will inherit it."*

> *Numbers 14:30-31 (AMP) "[30] Surely none shall come into the land in which I swore to make you dwell, **except Caleb** son of*

Jephunneh and Joshua son of Nun. [31] But your little ones whom you said would be a prey, them will I bring in and they shall know the land which you have despised and rejected. God said: 'Go and possess the Land.'"

Two men _____ **that**, regardless of the Giants in the land, regardless of their fortified cities, **the Lord was able to do what He said He would do.** They had faith to obey God. They added obedience to their faith in God. 40 years later we see them entering in the land promised them.

Numbers 26:64-65 (NIV) "[64] Not one of them was among those counted by Moses and Aaron the priest when they counted the Israelites in the Desert of Sinai. [65] For the LORD had told those Israelites they would surely die in the desert, and not one of them was left except Caleb son of Jephunneh and Joshua son of Nun."

I pray that God will fill our hearts with Faith to obey Him, to do everything He wants us to do for Him, so that in we might see the fulfilment of all that He Promised us.

How will we see the Good Promises fulfilled in our lives?

Persevere in Prayer and Trusting God

We need to learn from the Persistent woman who never gave up on making her requests known, until she was met with justice for her case.

Luke 18:1-8 (NIV) The Parable of the Persistent Widow [18:1] Then Jesus told his disciples a parable to show them that they should always pray and not give up. [2] He said: "In a certain town there was a judge who neither feared God nor cared about men. [3] And there was a widow in that town who kept coming to

him with the plea, 'Grant me justice against my adversary?' [4]
"For some time he refused. But finally, he said to himself, 'Even
though I don't fear God or care about men, [5] yet because this
widow keeps bothering me, I will see that she gets justice, so
that she won't eventually wear me out with her coming!'" [6]
And the Lord said, "Listen to what the unjust judge says. [7]
And will not God bring about justice for his chosen ones, who
cry out to him day and night? Will he keep putting them off?
[8] I tell you; he will see that they get justice, and quickly.
*However, when the Son of Man comes, **will he find faith on the***
earth?"

What kind of faith is required?

Faith to trust God for the impossible.

Every one of us know that God called us for a purpose. We will never
be fulfilled until we fulfill His purpose on our lives.

How many actually take that Call serious to Obey?

Romans 8:28 NIV "And we know that in all things God works for
the good of those who love him, who have been called according
to his purpose."

There are an ever-increasing amount of road rules, yet no one
gets in behind the steering wheel of a car and complains about
having to get on the road and having to obey every road rule and
every sign on the road, even though there might be many. You don't
complain every time you see a traffic light or stop sign and say: *"look,*
another one! Do I have to stop at every single traffic light, yield at every
single stop sign, obey every single road sign, even when no one might be
looking?" No, we know that it is in our best interest to obey the rules.

In our faith, in our walk with God, it is the same. **We need to add**
to our profession, _____, and faith to obey!

Whether that is in trusting God for **His provision**, when we stepped out by faith to tithe. Whether that is in trusting God **for salvation** in someone's life when we stepped out to share with them about God's Love for them and that He died for them. Whether it is trusting God for **justice**, or **Favour**, or **deliverance**, or **breakthrough**, or **reconciliation** or **restoration**, we apply faith to our obedience.

Whatever He asks you to do, be _____ and do it.

- _____ did what God asked him to do. *Judges chapters 6 to 9.*
- **The widow of Zarephath** acted on the Word when the prophet spoke to her. She received her miracle and never experienced famine again. All her debts was paid. *1 Kings 17 verses 9 to 16.*
- _____ did what the prophet told him to do. He applied obedience to his faith and received his _____. He was cured of leprosy. 2 Kings chapter 5.

Conclusion

In closing, let us make a decision today to _____ *God* and to _____ *Him*. This will ensure that the good work God started in our lives will be accomplished.

Hebrews 3:7-14 (NIV) Warning Against Unbelief "[7] So, as the Holy Spirit says: "Today, if you hear his voice, [8] do not harden your hearts as you did in the rebellion, during the time of testing in the desert, [9] where your fathers tested and tried me and for forty years saw what I did. [10] That is why I was angry with that generation, and I said, 'Their hearts are always going astray, and they have not known my ways.' [11] So I declared on oath in my anger, 'They shall never enter my rest.' [12] See to it, brothers, that none of you has a sinful,

unbelieving heart that turns away from the living God. [13] But
encourage one another daily, as long as it is called Today, so
that none of you may be hardened by sin's deceitfulness. [14]
We have come to share in Christ if we hold firmly till the end
the confidence, we had at first."

Let's have Faith to Obey God's Word!

Let us be that generation who benefit from the Word spoken into our
lives. May our obedience match the faith we profess.

Assimilation Sheet for
Faith and Obedience.

1. Complete the sentence. *Our first defence is to stay in a place of being full of the* _____.

2. What is the main message we derived from Hebrews chapter 4 verses 1 and 2. _____

_____

3. Complete the sentence. *The _____ of God is powerful and is full of _____, however these benefits are reserved for those who combine their faith with _____.*

4. What was Joshua and Caleb's report when they returned from spying out the Promised Land? Give Scriptural Proof. _____

_____

5. Joshua and Caleb pleaded with the people to go and take possession of the Land and not to rebel against the Lord. Where do we find this Pleading of Joshua and Caleb? _____

6. How many of the Twelve Spies, and How many of the people eventually entered the Promised Land? Provide Scriptural Reference.

_____

7. Name three other people who received their miracle because they combined obedience with their faith. Give Scriptures. _____

_____

8. Complete the sentence. *Let us make a decision today to _____ God and to _____ Him.*

PART II

OTHER BOOKS BY DR. HENDRIK J VORSTER

OTHER BOOKS BY DR HENDRIK J VORSTER

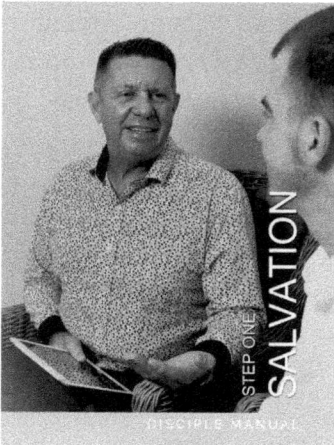

Discipleship Foundations - Step One - Salvation Disciple Manual

Step One - Salvation

This Course explores the "How to" be Born Again and to establish a solid Foundation for your faith in Jesus Christ. It is based on Hebrews chapter 6 verses 1 and 2, and explores:

Repentance of dead works,
Faith in God,
Baptisms,
Laying on of hands,
Resurrection of the dead, and
Eternal Judgement

Teacher Manuals and Video Teaching material are available from our website: www.churchplantinginstitute.com

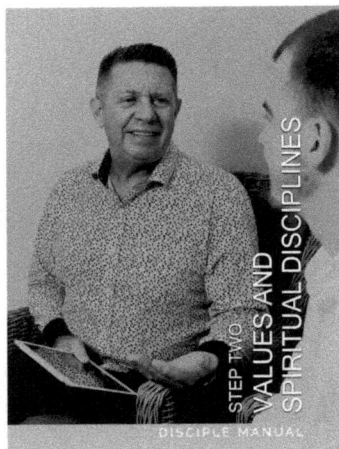

Discipleship Foundations Step Two - Values and Spiritual Disciplines Disciple Manual

Step Two - Values and Spiritual Disciplines Disciple Manual

This Course explores the "How to" develop spiritual disciplines as well as 52 Values Jesus taught. It is based on the teachings of Jesus to His Disciples, and explores:

Spiritual Disciplines

The disciplines we explore are: Reading, meditating on the Word of God, Prayer, Stewardship, Fasting, Servanthood, Simplicity, Worship, and Witnessing.

Values of the Kingdom of God

Humility, Mournfulness, meekness, Spiritual Passion, Mercifulness, Purity, Peacemaker, Patient endurance, Example, Custodian, Reconciliatory, Resoluteness, Loving, Discreetness, Forgiving, Kingdom of God Investor, God-minded, Kingdom of God prioritiser, Introspective, Persistent, Considerate, Conservative, Fruit-bearing, Practitioner, Accountability, Faithful, Childlikeness, Unity, Servanthood, Loyalty, Gratefulness, Stewardship, Obedience, Carefulness, Compassion, Caring, Confidence, Steadfastness, Contentment, Teachable, Deference, Diligence, Trustworthiness, Gentleness, Discernment, Truthfulness, Generous, Kindness, Watchfulness, Perseverance, Honouring and Submissive.

Teacher Manuals and Video Teaching material are available from our website: www.churchplantinginstitute.com

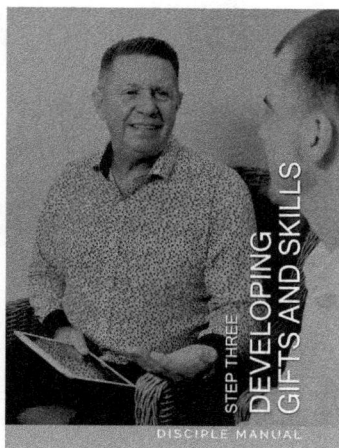

Discipleship Foundations Step Three - Developing Gifts and Skills

Step Three - Developing Gifts and Skills

This course is run through five weekend encounters. These weekend encounters have been designed to help Disciples discover their spiritual gifts, as well as learn skills to use their gifts, and to serve the Lord for the extension of His Kingdom. The Weekend Encounters are:

Gifts Discovery Weekend Encounter

We learn about Ministerial Office gifts, Service gifts, and Supernatural Spiritual Gifts. We discover our own, and then learn How we may use them to build up the local Church.

Survey of the Bible Weekend Encounter

During this weekend we do a survey of the Bible, from Genesis to Revelation. We also learn about the History of the Bible as well as How we can make most of our time in the Word.

Sharing your Faith Weekend Encounter

During this weekend we learn about the Gospel message, and How to share our faith effectively.

Overcoming Weekend Encounter

During this weekend we deal with those thistles and thorns that smother the growth and harvest of the good seed sown into our lives. We address How to overcome fear, unforgiveness, lust and the cares of the world with faith and obedience.

Shepherd Leader Weekend Encounter

During this weekend encounter we learn about being a Good Shepherd, and How to best disciple in a small group.

Teacher Manuals and Video Teaching material are available from our website: www.churchplantinginstitute.com

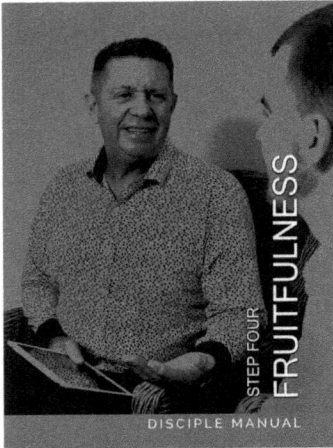

Discipleship Foundations Step Four - Fruitfulness

Step Four - Fruitfulness

We were saved to serve. This course has been designed to mobilise Believers from Learners to Practitioners. These sessions have been prepared for individual use with those who are producing fruit.

We explore:

1. Introduction.

2. Walking with purpose.

3. Build purposeful relationships. Finding Worthy Men

4. Priesthood. Praying effectively for those entrusted to you.

5. Caring compassionately.

6. Walking worthily.

7. Walking in the Spirit.

8. Practicing hospitality.

Teacher Manuals and Video Teaching material are available from our website: www.churchplantinginstitute.com

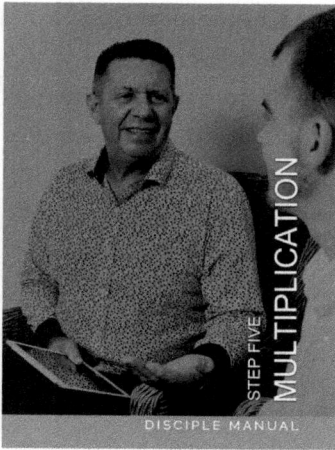

Discipleship Foundations Step Five - Multiplication

Step Five - Multiplication

This course was designed to assist fruit-producing disciples to live a life that will encourage a lifetime of fruitfulness. It will also give disciples skills and guidelines to navigate their disciples through seasons of challenge and growth. We explore:

1. Vision and dreams.
2. Set Godly Goals.
3. Character development
4. Gifts development
Impartation and Activation
5. Fruitfulness comes through constant challenge.
6. Relationships
Family, Children and Friends
7. The Power of encouragement
8. Finances
Personal and Ministry finances
9. Dealing with setbacks

- How to deal with failure?
- How to deal with betrayal?
- How to deal with rejection?
- How to deal with trials?
- How to deal with despondency?

10. Eternal rewards

Teacher Manuals and Video Teaching material are available from our website: www.churchplantinginstitute.com

VALUES

OF THE

KINGDOM

OF

GOD

Dr. Hendrik J. Vorster

Values of the Kingdom of God

By Dr. Hendrik J Vorster

Everyone desires to be known as a pleasant to be around with kind of person. This book helps you develop values towards such a godly character. This book explores 52 Values of the Kingdom of God.

Books are available from our website: www.churchplantinginstitute.com

SPIRITUAL
DISCIPLINES
OF THE
KINGDOM
OF
GOD

Spiritual Disciplines of the Kingdom of God

By Dr. Hendrik J Vorster

Every Believer desires to be a Fruit-producing branch in the Vineyard of our Lord. Developing spiritual disciplines is to develop spiritual roots from which our faith can draw sap to grow strong and fruit-bearing branches. This Book explores Nine Spiritual Disciplines of the Kingdom of God.

Books are available from our website: www.churchplantinginstitute.com

Church Planting

How to plant a dynamic church

Dr. Hendrik J. Vorster
Foreword by: Dr. Yonggi Cho

Church Planting - by Dr Hendrik J Vorster

Church Planting - How to plant a dynamic, disciple-making church
By Dr Hendrik J Vorster

This is a handbook for those who wish to plant a disciple-making church. This book explores every aspect of church planting, and is widely used in over 70 Nations on 6 Continents. Here is a list of the areas that are explored:

1. The challenge to plant New Churches
2. Phases of Church Planting
3. Phase One of Church Planting - The Calling, Vision and Preparation Phase
4. The Call to Church Planting
5. Twelve Characteristics of Church Planting Leaders
6. Church Planting Terminology
7. Phase Two of Church Planting - Discipleship
8. The Process of Discipleship
9. Phase Three of Church Planting - Congregating the Discipleship Groups
10. Understanding Church Planting Finances
11. Understanding Church staff
12. Phase Four of Church Planting - Ministry development and Church Launching Phase
13. Understanding and Implementing Systems
14. Phase Five of Church Planting - Multiplication
15. Understanding the challenges in Church Planting
16. How to succeed in Church Planting
17. How to plant a House Church

Student Manuals and Video Teaching material are available from our website: www.churchplantinginstitute.com

Discipleship Foundation Series on Video

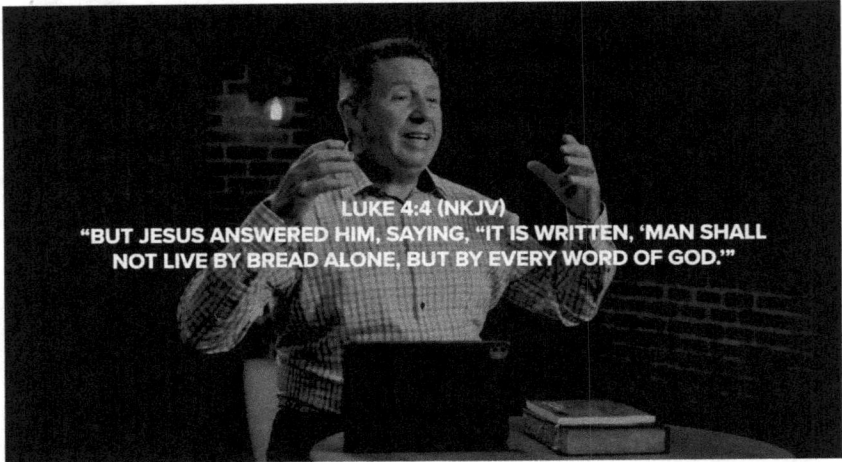

Dr. Vorster teaching via Video

185 Video Teachings are available for each of the Sessions taught throughout these Discipleship Courses.

Discipleship Foundation Series

We have Five, completely recorded, Discipleship Courses available on Video at www.discipleshipcourses.com

- **Step One - Salvation** (*This 7-week course helps the new Believer to establish, and build a solid Foundation for their faith to build on.*) This course is available, **without charge**, upon free registration.
- **Step Two - Values and Spiritual Disciplines** (*This 9-week Course helps the young Believer to put down Spiritual Roots, by establishing spiritual disciplines, and by learning the values of the Kingdom of God.*)
- **Step Three - Developing Gifts and Skills** (*This Course is usually presented during 5 Weekend Encounters, or over a 23-week period. We explore Spiritual Gifts and How to use them*

*to build up the local Church. We **explore the Bible**, and its origins, during one part to ensure we build our lives on the Handbook of the Bible. We also learn **How to share our faith.** We learn **How to deal with Strongholds** that might hold us back in fulfilling God's purpose. And finally, we learn **How to best Mentor** those whom we lead to Christ.)*

- **Step Four - Discipling Fruit-Producers** (*During this **8-week course** we learn How to teach our Disciples the principles that will develop, and maintain, fruitfulness.*)
- **Step Five - Multiplication** (*During this **11-week Course** we learn **How to Mentor our Leaders** to lead strong and healthy Fruit-producers.*)

Free registration for access to these Video resources is available at www.dicipleshipcourses.com

Church Planting Training Videos

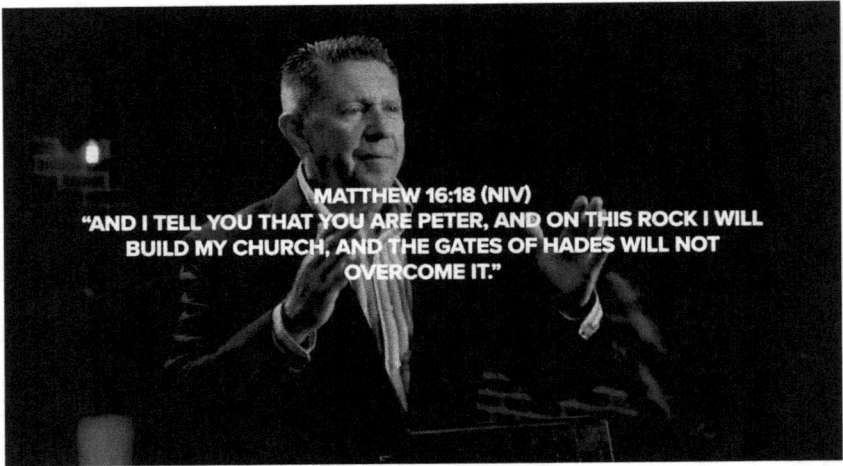

MATTHEW 16:18 (NIV)
"AND I TELL YOU THAT YOU ARE PETER, AND ON THIS ROCK I WILL
BUILD MY CHURCH, AND THE GATES OF HADES WILL NOT
OVERCOME IT."

Dr. Vorster teaching via Video

42 Video Teachings are available in this **Church Planting Course.**

- Introduction to Church Planting
- Why plant New Churches?
- Phases of Church Planting Overview
- Phase 1 - Preparation Phase
- Phase 2 - Team Building Phase
- Phase 3 - Prelaunch Phase
- Phase 4 - Launch Phase
- Phase 5 - Multiplication Phase
- Church Planting Trials
- Next Steps

Free Enrolment is available at www.churchplantingcourses.com

Advanced Coaching sessions are available for those who enrolled in the Masters Training Program.

ENDNOTES